Co

I thank the Almighty God for enabling me to write this book with the hope and prayer that this book will achieve its purpose as determined by God.

To my family for their support and encouragement.

Introduction

This book is special for you, you are highly favoured, chosen and honoured by your creator. He loves you more than anything, no matter who you are. He adores you and cares for you. So read this book with understanding and you will wonder what He really has for you. Indeed, you are a chosen individual for God.

Chapter 1

GOD'S LOVE FOR MANKIND

The subject of God's love is very vital to every human being. When we look back to the beginning of creation, God's love was loud and clear. We could see His love and compassion towards man, that we can be partakers of His blessedness and the glory of his image. What a wonderful God He is!

"Thou art worthy, O Lord, to receive glory and honour and power for thou hast created all things and for thy pleasure they are and were created." (Revelation 4:11). God is worthy to receive glory and honour for His benevolence which He has shown to man.

"The heavens declare the glory of God; and the firmament sheweth his handywork" (Psalms 19:1).

The creation of God is perfect and remarkable, no wonder the angels testify of His glory and creation,

"for His name alone is exalted, His splendour is above the earth and the heavens" (Psalms 148:13).

"*O Lord our Lord, how excellent is thy name in all the earth! who hast set thy glory above the heavens*" (Psalms 8:1).

"*In the beginning God created the heavens and the earth. And the earth was without form, and void, and darkness was upon the face of the deep. And the spirit of God moved upon the face of the waters. And God said, Let there be light: and there was light. And God saw the light, that it was good: and God divided the light from the darkness*" (Genesis 1:1-4).

Here the Bible states that: "God *divided the light from the darkness*". This "light" shows the image of God. God is light, there is no darkness in Him at all. For this point we know how God created heaven and earth with nothing, but the Spirit of God moved on the face of the waters and everything He commanded became reality.

This shows how amazing our God really is. This also proves that God has the power to do all things and He has glorious thoughts and plans for mankind. He created a happy environment for man to live in. Above all, He divided the light from the darkness so that we can live a normal life. A life without darkness or stumbling. *"Great peace have they which love thy law: and nothing shall offend them"* (Psalms 119:165). Indeed, great peace is for those who love God, and nothing will make them fall.

"For I know the thoughts that I think toward you, saith the Lord, thoughts of peace, and not of evil, to give you an expected end" (Jeremiah 29:11).

"And the Lord God said, it is not good that the man should be alone; I will make him an help meet for him." (Genesis 2:1).

God always has good intentions for man to satisfy us and also give us abundant life. Here we can see that God knows what is good and perfect for mankind to give us comfort, happiness, satisfaction, and an expected end.

God's love for man was demonstrated right from creation when He separated the light from the darkness. Following what we know so far, God's hope for man is that we can have fellowship with Him.

"*And God said, Let the earth bring forth grass, the herb yielding seed and the fruit tree yielding fruit after his kind, whose seed is in itself, upon the earth: and it was so. And the earth brought forth grass, and herb yielding seed after his kind, and the tree yielding fruit, whose seed was in itself, after his kind: and God saw that it was good*" (Genesis 1:11-12).

God is a wonderful Father, Redeemer, and Friend. A Father who loves and cares for His children, and creating a garden for man, that is beyond explanation. Look at that! God's thoughts and plans for mankind are unique. Who can do such a remarkable and wonderful thing for man? Only Almighty God can do that. That is how great our God is, His love and His uniqueness is unspeakable.

"*And the Lord God formed man of the dust of the ground and breathed into his nostrils the breath of life; and man became a living soul. And the Lord God planted a garden eastward in Eden; and there he put the man whom he had formed. And out of the ground made the Lord God to grow every tree that is pleasant to the sight, and good for food; the tree of life also in the midst of the garden, and the tree of knowledge of good and evil. And a river went out of Eden to water the garden; and from thence it was parted, and became into four heads*"* (Genesis 2:7-10). "*So God created man in his own image, in the image of God created he him; male and female created he them*" (Genesis 1:27).

Here we are looking at how God created man and also displayed the love He has towards us. God created man in His own image; perfect and beautiful like Himself. Also, that we can partake of His goodness and have fellowship with Him. That was God's plan for man and also that is what we were created for, not by accident but the original plan of God, the creator of the universe. The love of God shown here is infinite. He created a lovely, happy environment for us human beings to live in. You can see that in the garden where the elements of it or everything within it was beneficial to man. Every tree that was in the garden was edible and helped keep man healthy. Not only this, but it also created a beautiful scenery. This highlights the love and compassion God has for man and shows the care He has for man.

How amazing! All of God's plans and thoughts and creations are imaginative.

Who can understand how much God values man? "*For God so loved the world*". No wonder that He could do all these things for our good. Why can we not have a relationship with Him and reverence Him as the Saviour of our lives and also the whole world? We must endeavour to have a strong fellowship with God, the creator of heaven and earth. The I am that I am, the Almighty God.

"*Even every one that is called by my name: for I have created him for my glory, I have formed him; yea, I have made him*" (Isaiah 43:7). It states here that God created man for His own glory, so God wants man to come to Him as a Father and also a Creator.

"*Blessed is the man that trusteth in the Lord, and whose hope the Lord is. For he shall be as a tree planted by the waters, and that spreadeth out her roots by the river, and shall not see when heat cometh, but her leaf shall be green; and shall not be careful in the year of drought, neither shall cease from yielding fruit*" (Jeremiah 17:7-8).

No one who has demonstrated pure love or trust in our God has been disappointed. It has never happened, and it will never happen. God is love; His love is limitless.

Jeremiah 17:7-8, states, "*blessed is the man that trusted in the Lord and whose hope the Lord is*". This means trusting the Lord is not in vain and he goes on to say, "*for he shall be as a tree planted by the waters.*"

That person will flourish and never lack any good thing, because he has put his trust in the Lord. Furthermore, the person "*shall be like a tree planted by the rivers of water, that bringeth forth his fruit in his season; his leaf also shall not wither; and whatsoever he doeth shall prospe*r" (Psalm 1:3).

The Psalmist says the person who truly trusts in the Lord will be like a tree planted by the rivers of water. That individual will prosper, he or she will live with the abundance of all things; that is the plan of God for man.

"*A new commandment I give unto you, That ye love one another; as I have loved you, that ye also love one another*" (John 13:34). God has demonstrated pure and perfect love for you and me! He wants us to love Him too because He first loved man with perfect love. Therefore, we must love Him as well, that is the command from the Lord.

"*But my God shall supply all your needs according to his riches in glory by Christ Jesus*" (Philippians 4:19). "*He that spared not his own Son, but delivered him up for us all, how shall he not with him also freely give us all things?*" (Romans 8:32).

God can give us anything we desire if we will fully obey Him. Since He freely gave His only begotten Son for us, what will He not freely give to us? God can provide all that man needs because He can do all things. There is nothing that God who created heaven and earth cannot do. Jeremiah said, "*ah Lord God! behold, thou hast made the heaven and the earth by thy great power and stretched out arm, and there is nothing too hard for thee*" (Jeremiah 32:17). God Himself asked Jeremiah, "*behold, I am the Lord, the God of all flesh: is there anything too hard for me?*" (Jeremiah 32:27). There is absolutely nothing that our God cannot do! That is God! He will supply the needs of those who trust in Him, because He is rich in everything. Just come to Him with the humbleness of your heart and He will receive you.

God has promised to provide for those who seek Him; "*the young lions do lack and suffer hunger but they that seek the Lord shall not want any good thing*" (Psalm 34:10). God is saying that, those who trust in Him will lack absolutely nothing, that man will live in plenty. I encourage you to trust God and you will not be disappointed. If you seek Him, you will see His faithfulness.

"*Blessed are the merciful: for they shall obtain mercy*" (Matthew 5:7). You can obtain mercy only from the King of kings and Lord of lords. Come with a humble heart, and you will see God. All you need is a sincere heart, and you will definitely obtain mercy from the Lord.

"*But as many as received him, to them gave he power to become the sons of God, even to them that believe in his name: Which were born, not of blood, nor of the will of the flesh, nor of the will of man, but of God*" (John 1:12-13).

Therefore, if you are yet to believe, this is the right time to believe in His name, and you will become the son or daughter of God. Just like that, it will happen to you if you will believe in His name. As stated here, "But as many as receive Him, to them gave He power to become the sons of God." Is it not wonderful? He came to seek and to save those who are lost. *"And He shall be called Jesus: for He shall save His people from their sins"* (Matthew 1:21). Jesus said *"behold, I stand at the door and knock: if any man will hear my voice, and open the door, I will come in to him and will sup with him and he with me"* (Revelation 3:20). Will you open your heart for Jesus Christ to come in?

"Blessed are the pure in heart: for they shall see God" (Matthew 5:8). Do you want to see God as your Lord, Saviour and Redeemer? Then today is the perfect time for you! Do not hesitate to give Him your heart today and you will never regret it and you will never forget it either!

A song writer puts it this way:

Oh, what a wonderful, wonderful day

Day I will never forget

After I'd wandered in darkness away

Jesus my Saviour I met

Oh, what a tender compassionate Friend

He met the need of my heart

Shadows dispelling with joy I am telling

He made all the darkness depart.

That will be your portion in Jesus name. Amen

Chapter 2

GOD'S CARE FOR MANKIND

"The Lord is my shepherd; I shall not want. He maketh me to lie down in green pastures: he leadeth me beside the still waters. He restoreth my soul: he leadeth me in the paths of righteousness for his name's sake. Yea, though I walk through the valley of the shadow of death, I will fear no evil: for thou art with me; thy rod and thy staff they comfort me. Thou preparest a table before me in the presence of mine enemies: thou anointest my head with oil; my cup runneth over. Surely goodness and mercy shall follow me all the days of my life: and I will dwell in the house of the Lord forever" (Psalms 23:1-6).

God's care for human beings is spectacular! When you look at (Psalms 23:1), it says *"the Lord is my shepherd I shall not want"*. It means you will never lack anything. He will care for all your needs, in other words, He will look after you.

If God is taking care of you, what could possibly go wrong? He will provide for you. He will give you good health. He will make a way where there seems to be no way. He will make you the head and not the tail. He will take good care of you and your family. He will protect your going out and coming in and also perfect everything that concerns you.

Verse 2: "*He maketh me to lie down in green pastures: he leadeth me beside the still waters*" What is your need? Trust in the Almighty God and He will lead you into that particular thing you need. Do not doubt God. He always establishes what He has promised to do for those who trust Him. The Lord will lead you into all good things; physical, material, spiritual, and emotional needs. He is more than ready to do them. The Bible says God by "*His divine power hath given unto us all things that pertain unto life and godliness*" (2 Peter 1:3).

God will give you all what you need.

Verse 3: *"He restoreth my soul: he leadeth me in the paths of righteousness for his name's sake."* Are you sorrowful or hurt by someone? Do you have a broken heart? Come to Him and trust in His goodness and mercy that can never fail. He will restore peace and joy into your heart and will lead your soul into righteousness.

"Peace I leave with you, my peace I give unto you: not as the world giveth, give I unto you. Let not your heart be troubled, neither let it be afraid" (John 14:27).
Do not fear, believe in God, because He truly cares. *"Casting all your care upon Him; for He cares for you"* (1 Peter 5:7). God is the creator of your soul. He is ready to restore it to its original state and give you the perfect peace which passes all understanding.

Verse 4: *"Yea, though I walk through the valley of the shadow of death, I will fear no evil: for thou art with me; Thy rod and thy staff they comfort me."* Problems will be far from you because God will be with you, guide, and comfort you.

No matter what you are going through now, He can be trusted. His words are yea and amen. David from his young age to his adulthood acknowledged God's goodness, God's mercies, God's faithfulness, God's tender care and God's loving kindness. He was threatened, hated, and persecuted. He was even living in a cave and hunted by Saul, yet he put his hope in his maker, the God who can do all things and He delivered him from evil.

No wonder he wrote the testimony in (Psalms 23), because he was tested and now knows that the Lord is gracious.

"I will love thee, O Lord, my strength. The Lord is my rock, and my fortress, and my deliverer; my God, my strength, in whom I will trust; my buckler, and the horn of my salvation, and my high tower" (Psalms 18:1-2). Yes, God truly cares! He is faithful to everyone who calls upon His name and depends on Him as their creator and truly trust in Him wholeheartedly.

"Fear thou not; for I am with thee: be not dismayed; for I am thy God: I will strengthen thee; yea, I will help thee; yea, I will uphold thee with the right hand of my righteousness, For I the Lord thy God will hold thy right hand, saying unto thee, Fear not; I will help thee" (Isaiah 41:10,13). Here is the proof that, no matter how many hardships that come in our lives, God always reaches out to us and holds us firmly. He gathers and holds us in His strong and tender hands. Call upon Him in times of difficulty or if you are facing any problems and He will answer and deliver you from them all.

Verse 5: *"Thou preparest a table before me in the presence of mine enemies: thou anointest my head with oil; my cup runneth over."* God Almighty will prepare a banquet for you in the presence of those who hate you, those who do not like you, those who do not want to see your face and those who cause problems for you. He will make everything fall into place for you and you will not lack any good thing. You will be a blessing to others when your cup runs over.

Verse 6: "*Surely goodness and mercy shall follow me all the days of my life: and I will dwell in the house of the Lord forever.*"

Amen! Surely! Surely! God's goodness and His mercy will always follow those who call upon His name and believe Him. Obey His commands, depend on Him and His promises. Do that which is right in the sight of God and you will be in His presence for ever and ever, Amen.

"*One thing have I desired of the Lord, that will I seek after; that I may dwell in the house of the Lord all the days of my life, to behold the beauty of the Lord, and to enquire in his temple. I will sing, yea, I will sing praises unto the Lord*" (Psalms 27:4,6b).

Indeed, we will see the beauty of our Lord in our lives and also in time to come. Furthermore, we will sing praises for His marvellous work in our lives.

"For He hath said, I will never leave thee, nor forsake thee" (Hebrews 13:5b). God has made each one of us with His care and attention, committing himself to be involved in everything we go through. He has promised that "Never will I leave you; never will I forsake you". I will be with you and my right hand will uphold you.

"And God blessed them, and God said unto them, be fruitful, and multiply, and replenish the earth, and subdue it: and have dominion over the fish of the sea, and over the fowl of the air, and over every living thing that moveth upon the earth. And God said, Behold, I have given you every herb bearing seed, which is upon the face of all the earth, and every tree, in which is the fruit of a tree yielding seed; to you it shall be for meat." (Genesis 1:28-29).

God's plan for man is to care and bless us, as He said "Be fruitful, and multiply, and replenish the earth and subdue it". God's care for man is overwhelming! This shows that God cares for our wellbeing, because He has put all these things in place for us to enjoy them.

"And God blessed Noah and his sons, and said unto them, be fruitful, and multiply, and replenish the earth." "And you, be ye fruitful, and multiply; bring forth abundantly in the earth, and multiply therein" (Genesis 9:1,7). That is the will of God for man. He wants man to be blessed and happy in their lives, that was God's original plan for mankind.

In addition, He also wants us to have peace in our lives. *"Mercy unto you, and peace, and love, be multiplied."* (Jude 1:2). *"Saying, surely blessing I will bless thee, and multiplying I will multiply thee"* (Hebrews 6:14). This is the promise of God to mankind.

"And the Lord God took the man and put him into the garden of Eden to dress it and to keep it. And the Lord God commanded the man, saying, of every tree of the garden thou mayest freely eat" (Genesis 2: 15-16). Here it states God's great love and care for man. God commanded the man to freely eat from the trees in the garden; this was a great provision for man. Was it not awesome!

"And they heard the voice of the Lord God walking in the garden in the cool of the day: and Adam and his wife hid themselves from the presence of the Lord God amongst the trees of the garden. And the Lord God called unto Adam, and said unto him, Where art thou? And he said, I heard thy voice in the garden, and I was afraid (Genesis 3:8-10). God visited the man whom He put in the garden to see how they were doing. That shows God's precious love and concern for them, because He wants to know that everything was fine with them. Here we see the failure of man; they did not follow the instruction of God, because when they heard Him coming to the garden to have fellowship with them and also know their wellbeing, the Bible says, they

hid themselves. This was because they were afraid, they knew they did not obey the instruction God gave to them. But God, who is rich in love and mercy will still take good care of them, by providing immediate help for man.

My prayer is that we will appreciate God and value everything He has put in place for us. May God be with you all. Amen!

Chapter 3

GOD'S GIFT TO MANKIND

We all received gifts from our families, our friends, our loved ones, and many more, but the gift we are considering here supersedes the gifts we receive in our day to day lives. The extraordinary gift that only comes from God, the gift that changes man's life completely, the gift that sets man free, the gift that gives you hope for eternity, and the gift that stays with you forever, whether in memory or reality.

"For God so loved the world, that he gave his only begotten Son, that whosoever believeth in him should not perish, but have everlasting life" (John 3:16). This is the great invitation for everyone who is yet to know the Lord.

"In this was manifested the love of God toward us because that God sent his only begotten Son into the world, that we might live through him. Herein is love, not that we loved God, but that he loved us, and sent his Son to be the propitiation for our sins" (1 John 4:9-10). The Bible text tells us the love and compassion God has for man. Though we did not deserve such a great gift but by His unsearchable love and His grace towards man He has given to us freely.

"But God commendeth his love toward us, in that, while we were yet sinners, Christ died for us" (Romans 5:8). God has shown His love and care to man even when we sinned and disobeyed Him. He sent His Son to die in our place.

"For the wages of sin is death; but the gift of God is eternal life through Jesus Christ our Lord." (Romans 6:23). God's love for mankind is very unique and exceptional. He gave His only Son to die on the cross for man, so that we should not perish if we will believe in Him.

God has demonstrated clear love and compassion for man and how much He wants us to be blessed. That is the greatest gift. What a wonderful God we have! Every man must accept this precious gift.

Furthermore, God's love for man is unsearchable. He gave His only Son for our forgiveness and He paid the price for our sins so that we can be reunited with the Father again. Also, when we look at God's love for us, the amazing grace He has demonstrated to man and the strength He gives to us to live and do our day-to-day activities is great. The air we breathe, the protection we receive from Almighty God day after day is awesome, we should appreciate the provision and value them and love Him as Father and creator.

"Verily, verily, I say unto you, He that believeth on me hath everlasting life". (John 6:47). This is what the Lord Jesus Christ said, most assuredly if you believe in Him you will have everlasting life, with the sure promise. What are you waiting for? All these promises will happen to you, only if you will believe

in Him. What a gift! What a loving God!

"And the Lord God said, Behold, the man is become as one of us, to know good and evil: and now, lest he put forth his hand, and take also of the tree of life, and eat, and live forever: Therefore, the Lord God sent him forth from the garden of Eden, to till the ground from whence he was taken. So, he drove out the man; and he placed at the east of the garden of Eden Cherubims, and a flaming sword which turned every way, to keep the way of the tree of life" (Genesis 3:22-24).

The story here is a sad one, because God gave man all he needed to live a happy life in the garden of Eden, which means worry free. In other words, a Father provided everything His children could possibly need to live a happy life and commanded them to look after everything He had provided for them, but sadly they mishandled things. But when the Father found out He was displeased and corrected them. But He still loved and cared for them and gave man another opportunity to come to Him as their Father. He did not want man to suffer and perish.

He made provision for man to have a relationship with Him again, by sending His Son Jesus Christ as a gift to them, to atone for man's sins and reconcile them to God.

"God is faithful, by whom ye were called unto the fellowship of his Son Jesus Christ our Lord." (1 Corinthians 1:9). God is faithful and merciful. He has called man to have fellowship with Him and also with His Son Jesus Christ.

"All we like sheep have gone astray; we have turned everyone to his own way; and the Lord hath laid on him the iniquity of us all" (Isaiah 53:6).

"Every one of them is gone back: they are altogether become filthy; there is none that doeth good, no, not one" (Psalms 53:3).

"How then can man be justified with God? or how can he be clean that is born of a woman?" (Job 25:4). *"For all have sinned and come short of the glory of God; Being justified freely by his grace through the redemption that is in Christ Jesus"* (Romans 3:23-24).

It is only by receiving the gift of God, Jesus Christ as Lord and Saviour can man receive forgiveness and be reconciled with God.

"Have mercy upon me, O God, according to thy lovingkindness: according unto the multitude of thy tender mercies blot out my transgressions." (Psalms 51:1). Let that be your prayer if you are not a converted, born again child of God.

"Behold, I was shapen in iniquity; and in sin did my mother conceive me." (Psalms 51:5).

"But we are all as an unclean thing, and all our righteousnesses are as filthy rags; and we all do fade as a leaf; and our iniquities, like the wind, have taken us away" (Isaiah 64:6).

As a result of the failure and the mishandling of the garden of Eden and disobedience to God, where man sinned and came short of the glory of God, mankind has lost the love, peace, fellowship, protection, prosperity, and provision of God. But it is not the end of the world! God has given man another opportunity to call upon His name and be saved.

What a compassionate God we have! Just call upon Him today and He will answer you. Seek Him today and you will find Him.

"Come unto me, all ye that labour and are heavy laden, and I will give you rest" (Matthew 11:28). That is the call to salvation and rest from the labour of sin and ungodly living.

"Let us therefore come boldly unto the throne of grace, that we may obtain mercy, and find grace to help in time of need" (Hebrews 4:16).

Our Lord Jesus Christ is calling man to come to Him and He will give them rest, peace and joy for their souls.

"For the scripture saith, whosoever believeth on him shall not be ashamed. For there is no difference between the Jew and the Greek: for the same Lord over all is rich unto all that call upon him. For whosoever shall call upon the name of the Lord shall be saved" (Romans 10:11-13).

Amazing! Rich or poor, man or woman; whosoever shall call upon the name of the Lord will be saved! Do not miss or reject the greatest gift of all, that God is giving to you today. Appreciate the gift, accept the gift, and honour the gift of His only Son Jesus Christ and you will be saved. It is glorious to be a believer! Unto you first God, having raised up his Son Jesus, sent him to bless you, in turning away every one of you from his iniquities" (Acts 3:26). Receiving the gift of God, His Son Jesus Christ as Lord and Saviour, by repenting and turning away from your sins, will grant you forgiveness.

"*Much more then, being now justified by his blood, we shall be saved from wrath through him*" (Romans 5:9). "*And their sins and iniquities will I remember no more*" (Hebrew 10:17). When God forgives, He forgets. It is as if you have never sinned. "*Blessed are they whose iniquities are forgiven, and whose sins are covered*" (Romans 4:7). The shed blood of Jesus Christ will cover your sins and iniquities when you confess them and ask God for forgiveness.

"For God sent not his Son into the world to condemn the world; but that the world through him might be saved" (John 3:17).

Indeed, we shall be saved and have no more condemnation, because His grace is amazing and His love towards man is endless. So, if you will come to Him today, and accept Him as your Lord and Saviour, you will marvel at what God can do for you and through you.

You will have satisfaction
You will have joy
You will be blessed
You will have peace in your soul
You will be honoured
You will have treasure in heaven
You will be with the Lord in eternity.

Just come to Jesus, He will receive you just as you are! Rest your faith in Jesus Christ today. You do not need to pay or do anything, just come as you are, He is more than ready to welcome you. Jesus said, "*him that cometh to me I will in no wise cast out*" (John 6:37).

Just come to God, He will pardon and receive you as a precious son or daughter. How I pray that you reinforce this great privilege God has given you today. Amen.

Just as I am, without one plea,
But that Thy blood was shed for me,
And that Thou bidst me come to Thee,
O Lamb of God, I come! I come!

Just as I am, Thou wilt receive,
Wilt welcome, pardon, cleanse, relieve;
Because Thy promise I believe,
O Lamb of God, I come, I come!

Chapter 4

GOD'S CONCERN FOR MANKIND

As we have accepted the gift and called onto God, we have become the sons and daughters of God. The bible says, *"But as many as received Him, to them gave He power to become the sons of God, even to them that believe on His name"* (John 1:12).

"For ye are all the children of God by faith in Christ Jesus" (Galatians 3:2). *"Behold, God is my salvation; I will trust, and not be afraid: for the Lord Jehovah is my strength and my song; he also is become my salvation"* (Isaiah 12:2).

Here we know that we are the children of God by faith in Christ Jesus who died on the Cross of Calvary for our sins. We are new creatures in Christ Jesus. *"Saying, Amen: Blessing, and glory, and wisdom, and thanksgiving, and honour, and power, and might, be unto our God for ever and ever. Amen"* (Revelation 7:12).

God's concern for His children or believers is great. His love and compassion for believers is that they will be with Him in eternity. He wants those who are saved and have put their trust in Him to be with Him in heaven and live with Him forever.

That was the prayer of our Lord Jesus Chris when He said, "*Father, I will that they also, whom thou hast given me, be with me where I am; that they may behold my glory, which thou hast given me: for thou lovedst me before the foundation of the world*" (John 17:24). "*In hope of eternal life, which God, that cannot lie, promised before the world began*"
(Titus 1:2). This is the sure promise from our Father, God that cannot lie. "*God is not a man that He should lie*" (Numbers 23:19). His yes is yes, and no is no. Jesus wants us to see the glory which His Father has given to Him. He wants us to enjoy that glory with Him. He does not want us to suffer in this world. This world is full of hatred, pain, troubles, fears, hardship, trials, uncertainty, sicknesses, confusion, wickedness and many more.

But Jesus Christ specifically promised those who believe in Him that He is going to prepare a peaceful place for them, and He will come and take us with Him, so that where He is, we will be there also.

"Let not your heart be troubled: ye believe in God, believe also in me. In my Father's house are many mansions: if it were not so, I would have told you. I am going to prepare a place for you. And if I go and prepare a place for you, I will come again, and receive you unto myself; that where I am, there ye may be also" (John 14:1-3).

Here is the promise that our Lord Jesus Christ has made to all believers, encouraging believers to not worry about anything but that they should instead trust in God and also in Him. When He says that there are many mansions in His Father's house, He means what He says, and we cannot compare the mansions in heaven with anything we know on earth.

"*Ah Lord God! behold, thou hast made the heaven and the earth by thy great power and stretched out arm, and there is nothing too hard for thee*" (Jeremiah 32:17).

There is a big yes, there is nothing God who created the universe cannot do. He can do all things. Just believe in Him, just trust in his name, He is taking us to a place we never, never dreamt of; a place with surprises, a place with breath taking beauty, a place with astonishment, a place with excitement and a place with happiness, where we can see all believers who have gone before us. Isn't it beautiful? Heaven is a glorious, perfect, happy home for all believers. This is our strength and hope, so every believer must endeavour to watch and wait till He comes. It is a great opportunity for us to spend remarkable time with our Lord and Saviour in heaven.

"*Whereby are given unto us exceeding great and precious promises: that by these ye might be partakers of the divine nature, having escaped the corruption that is in the world through lust*" (2 Peter 1:4).

We are made to enjoy the divine nature of our Lord. This shows just how awesome our God truly is. We shall be like Him here on earth and in heaven.

"*For we which have believed do enter into rest, as he said, As I have sworn in my wrath, if they shall enter into my rest: although the works were finished from the foundation of the world*" (Hebrews 4:3). We that have believed in the name of Jesus Christ, will enter into His rest. No doubt about that. We will rest from our labours.

"*For the Lamb which is in the midst of the throne shall feed them and shall lead them unto living fountains of waters: and God shall wipe away all tears from their eyes*" (Revelation 7:17). Oh yes, all tears will be wiped away. "*And there shall be no more death, neither sorrow, nor crying, neither shall there be any more pain: for the former things are passed away*" (Revelation 21:4).

"*He hath made the earth by his power, he hath established the world by his wisdom, and hath stretched out the heaven by his understanding*" (Jeremiah 51:15). Here we learn about God's power, wisdom and understanding. It is very hard for one to explain God's power, wisdom and understanding, it is a mystery. "*To the only wise God our Saviour, be glory and majesty, dominion, and power, both now and ever. Amen*" (Jude1:25).

But Heaven will be fabulous, please try to be there. Are you a believer? Then endure to the end. Be ready and watch for His coming. Are you not a believer yet? Surrender your life to Jesus and receive Him as Lord and Saviour?

"*But as it is written, Eye hath not seen, nor ear heard, neither have entered into the heart of man, the things which God hath prepared for them that love him*" (1 Corinthians 2:9). Indeed, God has prepared something indescribable for them that love Him. No wonder the Bible states, "eye have not seen, nor ear heard".

Yes, it is beyond words. In other words, no mind can imagine what the Almighty God has prepared for those who truly love Him. If you are not yet a believer, it is not too late, just come to the Lord today and He will receive you with open arms.

He said *"Behold, I stand at the door, and knock: if any man hear my voice, and open the door, I will come in to him, and will sup with him, and he with me"* (Revelation 3:20).

You can become one of the lucky ones if you believe in Him. It can be possible if you just come to Him in faith and He will receive you, so that you can enjoy His provisions and also become a partaker of His goodness and blessings. Nothing matters more than being with your Creator and Redeemer in heaven.

"Beloved, now are we the sons of God, and it doth not yet appear what we shall be: but we know that, when he shall appear, we shall be like him; for we shall see him as he is" (1John 3:2). What a glorious moment it will be.

It will be as the hymn writer wrote:

> When we all get to heaven,
>
> What a day of rejoicing that will be!
>
> When we all see Jesus,
>
> We'll sing and shout the victory!

"And God shall wipe away all tears from their eyes; and there shall be no more death, neither sorrow, nor crying, neither shall there be any more pain: for the former things are passed away" (Revelation 21:4). Heaven is worry-free. Can you imagine that? We are going to rest in His presence. There is no crying, no pain, no hatred because all the former things will pass away.

"Thine eyes shall see the king in his beauty: they shall hold the land that is very far off" (Isaiah 33:17). This is the promise that Isaiah has shared from God to everyone who is saved through faith. We will see Jesus Christ the King in all His glory. Every serious believer is going to see a land that is very far off. This is our hope and prayer to see Jesus Himself, and to be with Him forever.

"Keep yourselves in the love of God, looking for the mercy of our Lord Jesus Christ unto eternal life."
(Jude 1:21). We will keep ourselves in the love of God and follow Him daily to guide us into eternal life. We will not fall on the wayside. We will not deviate from righteousness and holiness. We will keep and obey His commandments in love.

"Which in his times He shall shew, who is the blessed and only potentate, the King of kings, and Lord of lords. Who only hath immortality, dwelling in the light which no man can approach unto, whom no man hath seen, nor can see, to whom be honour and power everlasting. Amen" (1 Timothy 6:15-16).
Now we know the unlimited power and glory of our Lord Jesus Christ and His blessedness. Heaven will be glorious. All the joy we are to have in heaven will come from the presence of the Almighty God. God's presence will be the light and the life in heaven and also God's Spirit will be felt everywhere. Here it gives believers on earth a great goal to reach and it creates an image of the perfectness of our Lord Jesus Christ.

But how sweet will it be when we see God face to face as He is? It will be unspeakable. Will we forget all the things that we have passed through in our lives here on earth? No one knows. Oh yes, we will. Paul wrote, *"for I reckon that the suffering of this present time are not worthy to be compared with the glory which shall be revealed in us"* (Romans 8:18).

Let us therefore endure afflictions, hardness, persecution, scorning, run the Christian race to the end, fight as good soldiers of the Lord and keep the faith. We will say like Apostle Paul at the end of our lives, *"I have fought a good fight, I have finished my course, I have kept the faith"* (2 Timothy 4:7). We will not miss the crown. The Lord Himself will keep us from falling.

"Blessed be the God and Father of our Lord Jesus Christ, which according to his abundant mercy hath begotten us again unto a lively hope by the resurrection of Jesus Christ from the dead, to an inheritance incorruptible, and undefiled, and that fadeth not away, reserved in heaven for you.

Who are kept by the power of God through faith unto salvation ready to be revealed in the last time" (1 Peter 1:3-5).

We thank the Lord for showing His love, mercy, goodness, and care upon us, to receive us unto Himself again, and also given us the opportunity to be partakers of His heavenly glory and everlasting kingdom. Now that we are the children of the most high God, we must obey Him in everything and also live holy and righteous lives. By doing that, we will maintain a strong relationship with Him. As we know, God requires total obedience from all His children and nothing less.

His grace is sufficient for us, let us hold firmly onto Him and lean on His gentle arms and He will surely see us through. The grace of God be with you all and we will meet in heaven. Amen.

Conclusion

We thank God for His infinite love and amazing grace and mercy He has shown to mankind and accepting us to Himself again. He has also made us to be partakers of his heavenly blessings.

His love, goodness, mercy, and care towards us are beyond words and all I can say is that indeed He is truly Abba Father. God has great care and unsearchable love for man, even when we missed the mark and disobeyed Him. He shown compassion for us and sent His only Son Jesus Christ to die for us, so that the fellowship that we

lost with the Father can be restored again through our Lord Jesus Christ by faith. We praise God for His glorious love for us.

"All we like sheep have gone astray; we have turned everyone to his own way; and the Lord hath laid on him the iniquity of us all" (Isaiah 53:6).

We bless the name of our Lord for His benevolence, care and concern for man and what God has done for us and what He is still going to do in our individual lives. He is omnipotent and can do all things. Let us appreciate His works in our lives and have great faith in Him. He will establish what He has promised to us and more than we ourselves are expecting.

May His word be rich in our hearts and minds, in Jesus' Mighty name, Amen.

Prayer

Everlasting God I thank you for showing compassion for me and for sending your Son Jesus Christ to the Cross of Calvary to die in my place. I come to you today and I acknowledge my sin.

Please forgive me for all my sins. I know that only you can forgive me and write my name in the Book of Life. "*For I acknowledge my transgressions: and my sin is ever before me*" (Psalms 51:3). Please forgive me all my sins. I repent and renounce every sin in my life. I receive you as my Lord and Saviour. Because "*Neither is there salvation in any other: for there is none other name under heaven given among men, whereby we must be saved.*" (Acts 4:12).

I thank you very much Lord Jesus Christ for giving me that opportunity and saving my soul from the Lake of Fire and by your special grace I am now free from condemnation. Now I am a child of God and I am a new creature in Christ Jesus.

Thank you, God, for your unsearchable and indescribable love. I promise to live and serve you to the end. In Jesus' name I pray, Amen.

Printed in Great Britain
by Amazon